Excel:

QuickStart Guide - From Beginner to Expert

D0169950

7-16-16

William Fischer

Introduction

William Fischer

attempt has been made to provide accurate, up to date and reliable complete information. No warranties of any kind are expressed or implied. Readers acknowledge that the author is not engaging in the rendering of legal, financial, medical or professional advice.

By reading this document, the reader agrees that under no circumstances are we responsible for any losses, direct or indirect, which are incurred as a result of the use of information contained within this document, including, but not limited to, —errors, omissions, or inaccuracies.

Introduction

Haven't you ever seen a catalogue that is so beautifully arranged you want to create one just like it? A statistical report that intelligently updates itself whenever some changes are made? A colorful and easily readable chart that can automatically adjust itself to the latest changes? All of these are possible with the help of the most widely used spreadsheet software Microsoft Excel.

With an Excel spreadsheet, you can organize large amounts of data that look initially meaningless and convert them to useful information, on which you can additionally perform mathematical operations. Microsoft was one of the first to create user-friendly interfaces, so you can imagine how easy Excel would be, even if you have got absolutely no idea about it. Designed for quick calculations, managing data, creating charts, and basically performing any kind of operation on the data, MS Excel is one of the best out there. It became the industry standard spreadsheet. Previously, Lotus 1-2-3 held the standard, but the ease, power, and versatility of Excel helped it replace Lotus 1-2-3. Usually, powerful tools are very complicated to use, but Microsoft proved that this was not the case with Excel.

Being a Microsoft product, you may think that Excel is available only in Windows systems and devices. This is not true, Excel is available in Windows, Mac, iOS, and Android.

Excel 2016 can be effectively used even in touch devices such as your smartphones or tablets, without any issues. The versions after 2010 all have added immense support to sharing files, and you can now work on the same document in different devices at different times.

As a computer program, Microsoft Excel has existed for many years. It has been a significant part of a working professional's arsenal since the 1990s and has been steadily growing in popularity up to now. In this book, you will learn more about what Microsoft Excel truly is and how it can help you become the most efficient office professional you can be.

Starting with Excel 2.0 (there never was 1.0 version), Microsoft has continued to update its version, every year or two, including a wide variety of features that kept Excel at the top of the leading spreadsheet software. The most significant change was made in 2007, with Excel 2007 having a completely different layout than the Excel 2003. The ribbon, which is the go-to spot for different commands, came to be greatly appreciated due to its simplicity. Excel 2010 and 2013 saw more updates to improve multi-threading and new functions. Finally, 2016 came with a large number of new charts, and stability improvements.

This book will focus on key aspects of Excel, to help you become an expert in a matter of hours. That's right! A few hours of dedication is all you need to truly master Excel and its multitude of features. The entire book assumes you are using MS Excel 2013. If you have the 2016 version, do not worry, this book can still be used, as almost all the features of the 2013 versions are available on the 2016 version. A separate chapter has been added to highlight the differences between Excel 2016 and Excel 2013.

It is also my hope that through this book, you will learn how to realize fully the program's potential to become even more useful to you. Some people may say that this particular program is one of the hardest to understand because of the complicated formulas required to operate Excel. However, I can assure you that Excel is the easiest to manage once you truly understand how it works. For this reason, I urge you to turn the page and read on to learn more about this fascinating program.

William Fischer

Chapter 1: The Basics

What is Microsoft Excel?

Microsoft Excel refers to a spreadsheet application that was developed by the Microsoft Company for Windows, along with other related programs and operating systems. With this program, you will be able to calculate different values as well as to form tables. It also has various graphing tools that can be handy in the long run when solving different scientific and mathematical formulas.

Excel has been widely used by computer experts around the world since 1993. As mentioned earlier, it has even replaced Lotus 123 as a standard for spreadsheet creation and computerized computation. The subsequent paragraphs will discuss more the nature of this program and how it works. We will discuss how the different functions and charts can help you report or analyze data in the most appropriate way.

The key uses of Excel include organizing and representing the collected information or data as charts, graphs, and tables. When you want to organize large amounts of data and manage it properly, you need Excel. You can integrate information from different files, and analyze them effectively (and easily) with Excel.

Instead of giving detailed information on things that are obvious like the blank space you're working on, this section will focus more on the features of Excel that you really need to know about.

When you enter data into a cell in the spreadsheet, you might notice that the same data appears on a bar on the top. This bar is called the **Formula bar**, and you will be making use of this bar quite often. Any changes made in the formula bar of a specific cell will be reflected back on the cell itself, and vice-versa.

Let us now head straight into some of the most basic features of Excel should know to move from a beginner to an expert.

The Ribbon

The Microsoft Office Excel ribbon is your personal Excel tour guide. Anything you want to accomplish with Excel, you can do it with the ribbon's multitude of options. The only problem, however, is that it is extremely difficult to try and remember a specific where a particular function, format, or option is, considering the fact that there are 8 tabs! This is especially true if you are just a beginner. With that said, the ribbon was actually implemented to make things easier. That's right! Prior to 2007, all the MS Office software had just toolbars. No easily accessible tabs and no images on the different functions. Can you imagine working on a worksheet like that? Especially when you're just starting out and have no clue where anything is? This is where the ribbon came to the rescue. Images were added to different functions so that the user interface was as friendly as possible.

When you do get used to the ribbon, you will find it extremely easy to perform different functions and create unique formats. When you don't remember a particular function or the shortcut for a particular task, then the ribbon will be your savior. Backtracking to the structure of the ribbon, it has three main parts (which makes or breaks your spreadsheet):

- Tabs
- Groups
- Commands

Tabs: At the very top of the spreadsheet, you will be able to see 8 tabs, with the **File** tab always selected by default. These tabs contain groups of commands that are related to each other. For example, under **Insert** you will be having options to insert a graph, insert a chart, and so on and so forth.

Groups: When groups were mentioned before, what was meant was an actual component of the ribbon called a group? Each group has related commands, and the name of each group appears at the bottom of the group, below the tab. For example, in the group **Alignment** under the **Home** tab, you have several options of alignments to choose between (the left, centre, or justified).

Commands: These are the actual commands you will be using. Each command performs a specified function, and the number of commands available are so diverse that you can practically do anything you want to with your ideas and creativity being the only limitation.

When you look at the tabs and the ribbons, you may feel that they are organized quite the way you want them to be. Fret not, because you have been given the power to customize the ribbon the way you want to make it *your* ribbon. The following section will explain about customizing a ribbon to truly make it your own, and to make it much easier for you to apply certain commands if you will be using them more than the others.

Customizing the Ribbon

First things first, if the ribbon is quite what you want of if the space that the ribbon occupies is what you're looking for, then you can just collapse the ribbon. That's right, you can make the ribbon disappear (and bring it back whenever you feel like it). Do the following to collapse the ribbon:

Right click on the ribbon area (it can be anywhere within the ribbon). Click on **Minimize the Ribbon**.

Now the ribbon would have disappeared from the screen. They haven't disappeared forever; you just need to click on each tab whenever you want to make use of some command. Whenever you click the tab, the commands do appear, albeit temporarily. As soon as you are done with the commands, they automatically disappear, giving you the minimized look once again. Unfortunately, the same also happens as soon as you click somewhere within the document, before applying the command. You have to be careful to not mis-click anywhere before applying the commands you want to. With that out of the way, if you still want to customize the ribbon, read on:

- Right click on the ribbon area.
- Click on **Customize the Ribbon**.

Now a (not-so-little) dialog box should pop up. Now, suppose you want to create a tab with specific groups in mind. And suppose in the default ribbon, these groups are spread across various tabs, which you do not want to select each time you are in need of a particular command. Do the following to create a new tab with your own customized commands:

- Click on **New Tab**
- Go ahead and create a name for your tab.
- Select the command you want to add to your tab, then click on **Add** button in the centre.
- In order to remove certain commands from a tab, click on the required command, then click on **Remove** which is just below the Add.
- Now your tab appears in Ribbon, along with the other tabs (which you can customize as well).
- If you do not want a particular group to be present in the ribbon, just uncheck it in the Customize Ribbon dialog box.

Apart from just creating tabs, you can even create new groups. Creating groups is just as easy as creating tabs is.

- Click on **New Group**
- Name the group, as you like.
- If your tab contains multiple groups, you can select which group you want the particular command to be in. Add the command by clicking on the **Add** button or remove it with the **Remove** button.

The created groups also appear in the tab you have created, along with the other tabs (if you have customized one of the default tabs).

Importing and Exporting

Instead of customizing your own Ribbon after seeing someone else's, you can just import their customization. Take care that you export your current ribbon customizations first before importing, or you will permanently lose it.

- Go to the **Customize the Ribbon** window.
- Click on **Import/Export**
- To import a file, click on **Import customization file.**
- To export your customization, click on **Export all customizations.**

Resetting the Ribbon

The occasion may also arise where you may need to delete all your customizations and reset everything, bringing it back to the default settings. Though not often, this is usually done when the ribbon you have customized gets bugged and stops applying the right commands. To reset the customizations, this is what you have to do:

- Head to the Customize Ribbon dialog box.
- Click on **Reset**.
- Select **Reset all customizations**.

It's important for you to note that *this resets both the Ribbon customizations and the Quick Access Toolbar customizations*. If you do not want your quick access toolbar customizations (as explained in the next section) to be deleted as well, then be careful here.

Quick Access Toolbar

Notice the tiny toolbar above the Ribbon's File Tab? It's extremely easy to miss, and has only **Undo, Redo, and Save**, leading to most people thinking it's just another bar of not much importance. This is the Quick Access Toolbar or QAT.

When you're using Excel extensively and need to use a couple of commands repeatedly, then going for the Quick Access Toolbar instead of clicking on the corresponding tab and group may be faster. It also acts as a substitute for a customized Ribbon. For example, you can have a few alignment options in your Quick Access Toolbar while having your Insert tab open and ready to insert pictures or charts at any given time. The best part is, once you get used to using the Quick Access Toolbar, you will start to depend less on the Ribbon.

Are those 3 default commands the only ones you can use with the QAT? Definitely not. With the small drop-down button at the right end of the QAT (**Customize the Quick Access Toolbar**), the most widely used commands appear, from which you can select anything you want. You are also not confined to the displayed 12 commands. Just click on **More Commands** and you will be able to choose from all the commands available.

When you need to add a command that is not available in the Ribbon, then:

- Go to **Customize the Quick Access Toolbar**.
- Click on **More Commands**
- Under the **Choose Commands from** dropdown list, select **Commands Not in the Ribbon**.

You can now select whichever command you want to the QAT.

If you feel like adding a command on the go while you're

working on a particular spreadsheet, just do this:

- **Right click** the command.
- Select **Add to Quick Access Toolbar**

With this, the command you just selected will now appear on the right side.

Limitations

The QAT however, does have limitations. If you select the **Font type** command, then clicking on the QAT will only open the Font list, and you cannot add a particular font to the QAT. The QAT also cannot be placed anywhere you like. There are only two fixed spots that you can choose from. The first is just above the **File** tab in the Ribbon, then second is just below the Ribbon.

When the time comes where you rely more on the QAT than the tabs for picking out specific commands, you might want to think about shifting the QAT to below the Ribbon. This brings it closer to the workspace. Simple **Right click the QAT -> Show below Ribbon**. This should push the QAT below the Ribbon.

Customizing QAT

Seeing as how you're limited to having only one seventh of all the commands open at a time, the QAT can help you use commands from multiple tabs, from a single location. You can further enhance its functionality, by customizing it.

- **Right click** the QAT.

- Click on **Customize Quick Access Toolbar**

This opens the Excel Options dialog box, and like the Ribbon Customization, the QAT Customization will be selected

Creating Sections

You can create sections of commands in your QAT (though it's not possible to create groups like in tabs), with the help of some customizations. Select the **Popular Commands** under the **Choose Commands from** list. Click on **<Separator>** and then click on **Add**. This will create a section, wherever you place it. To place the separator where you want, click the **Move up** and **Move down** arrow.

With this, you can further organize your QAT by making it look like it actually has groups, but just contains the commands separated by a small space.

Changing the Order

When you decide to add commands one-by-one into the QAT,

they get added in order. You can change this order easily to your liking by following this:

- Click on **File** tab.
- Click on **Options** under the **Help** tab.
- Click on **Quick Access Toolbar**.

Here, you can make whatever changes you want, including changing the order of the commands as they appear on the screen.

Importing/Exporting a QAT

You may sometimes feel the need to get the same QAT layout that a friend or a co-worker has if it's more convenient. Instead of copying the same QAT by customizing it yourself, you can just import the QAT. Do the following to import a QAT:

- Click on **File** tab.
- Click on **Options** under the **Help** tab.
- Click on **Quick Access Toolbar**.
- Now click on **Import/Export**.
- To import, select **Import customization file**.
- To export, select **Export customization file**.

Exporting your QAT should pose no issues, but you have to be careful while importing. Whenever you import a customization file, *your* customization disappears, forever.

The only way of saving your previous customization is by exporting it to another system, and then importing it whenever you feel the need to switch again.

Formatting

Under Formatting lies an ocean of possibilities that can make your Excel spreadsheet look better and unique in the hundreds of others out there with similar data. Formatting does not simply include you changing your Font type, and Font size or color. Excel allows you to format the cells and tables of your workbook in any way you want. You can format a group of cells, you can format every cell, and you can format a single cell. Excel gives you the power to make your spreadsheet look just the way you want it to.

It's not just about how presentable your spreadsheet is. When you have enormous amounts of data stored in your spreadsheet, it becomes near impossible to go through it without getting confused. You need to format different sections of the spreadsheet so that you know where each data is located.

Formatting Cells

This bonus feature of Excel 2013 will allow you to identify various points of interest in your worksheet. You can activate this feature by going to the home tab in the taskbar and selecting the range of cells that you would want to highlight. After this, click on the drop down menu then go into the Highlight Cells Rules menu.

You should have already known by now, but a cell is the individual box that is located throughout your spreadsheet. You name a cell by its column and row. The rows are numbered, whereas the columns are lettered. Assuming you're talking about the 5th column and the 4th row, the corresponding cell is name **E4.** It sounds quite obvious, and will not be discussed in detail further.

Cell Formatting is the first thing you need to know about when it comes to making your spreadsheet look organized. It is very easy to use the different formatting options because they are all grouped under a single option:

Select the cell (or cells) you want to format.
- **Right click -> Format Cells**.
- This opens a **Format Cells** dialog box, where you have options to format the **Number, Alignment, Font, Border, Fill,** and **Protection.** (More on protection later).

A good example of the use of this feature would be if you are scoring tests and want to highlight the scores in red. Traditionally, you will use the red text or light red fill to highlight the cells that you would need. However, with conditional formatting, you will not have to do it manually anymore. Another example would be if you wanted to highlight certain parts of your document with higher numerical results than others. The applications for this feature are almost endless.

You can also create many different rules for different cells and worksheets using this particular characteristic. Excel 2013 also has a Custom Format function that will individually change the structure of each cell depending on what you need.

This unique trait is why Excel is deemed to be the most dynamic and useful computer programs that Microsoft has ever created. It will not only make your life with charts easier to handle, but it will also make the task even more enjoyable.

Let us now take a look at some of the most important formatting available in Excel:

Font Size, Color, and Type

The most basic type of formatting, you are allowed to change the appearance of the text or numbers in your cells as you like.

To change your font color or size or type, click on the **Fonts** tab. Make the necessary changes using the different drop down list boxes. The good thing here is that you do not need to try out different styles and apply changes to see which suits your needs better. Excel displays a preview of the font change you have just made, and you can just keep switching styles till you see the one that feels just about right.

If you feel going to the Format Cells dialog box is tedious to do every time to change font styles or color, just go to the **Home tab.** Here, the **Font group** (which is present by default) contains the exact same options that the dialog box did. Just make the changes here.

Number

The default number category that Excel has on all its cells is the **General** type. Whatever number you type appears as is, without any changes. You can, however, change it to display a specific currency, or a date, or a fraction.

For example, let us take currency. Select a particular cell, then go to **Format Cells**. Click on **Currency** in the **Number tab**, and then select the number of decimal places and the symbol. Suppose you select 3 decimal places, with the **£** symbol. You can see that the preview shows **£1234.000**. This is exactly how the number in the cell would look like. If you now type in any number, it will be preceded by £, and succeeded by 3 decimal places.

Sometimes, you are not required to specify the category of the cell yourself. Excel is intelligent enough to figure what it is that you are entering into the cell, and it changes the cell category according. For example, typing **5 1/2** automatically changes that cell's category to **Fraction**. Typing **%** after a number will automatically change its category to the **Percentage**.

Border

Borders can be used to highlight certain parts of the spreadsheet, or to make it look different in general.

- Select the cell (or range of cells) over which you wish to place a border.
- **Right click -> Format Cells**.
- Click on **Border** tab.
- Click on **Outline** if you want only the outer edges of the group of cells to be bordered.
- Click on **Inside** if you want each cell to bordered as well.

Borders are not limited to just thickening of the already present thin lines. You can select from a range of available options like the double line, hashed line, thickened line, and so on and so forth. Choose the border, choose the color from the drop down list box, and apply the necessary the changes. Once again, Excel makes your job easier by giving you a preview of how the border would look like.

If you want specific portions to be bordered, you can simply click on the preview image. Click the part where you want the border to be placed, and it automatically appears. This is much better when you want to apply a unique border style.

Protection

With large amounts of data stored in a single spreadsheet comes the added risk of insecurity. You want your data to be present, you can't make any changes to that, but you don't want anyone else editing your well-organized spreadsheet. The only way for this to happen is by protecting your spreadsheet. MS Excel gives you of the option of protecting your cells from unauthorized changes. Of course, this means you have to protect your spreadsheet itself first, or there would be no meaning.

So let us take a look at how you can protect your spreadsheet first:

- Click on the **Review tab.**
- Now click on the **Protect Sheet** button.
- In the **Protect Sheets** window, type in a password, and click on OK.

Your spreadsheet is now protected. You now have to unprotect all your cells first, before being able to lock them.

- Select the entire spreadsheet.
- **Right click -> Format Cells.**
- Select **Protection** tab.
- Uncheck the locked and hidden boxes if it's already checked.

You can now go ahead and lock and hide your cells so that

the wrong hands will not be able to change it.

- Select the cells (or cells) you want to protect.
- Go back to the same **Protection** tab.
- Click on the **Locked** and **Hidden** checkboxes.

When cells are locked, only the people who know the password to your spreadsheet will be able to make any changes. Hiding the cell contents means that you are not showing the person without the password the formulas you have used on a particular cell.

To Summarize

With the amount of sensitive data encoded into Excel spreadsheets, it is imperative to use every measure to ensure the safety and security of the data from hackers and possible cyber attacks in the future. This problem is why the program is password enabled with password creation offered for the following actions:

- Document security
- Document modification
- Worksheet protection and vice versa
- Workbook protection
- Protection from sharing workbook data

Because of password protection, this security and safety of all documents in Excel are ensured. You will not have to worry about your calculations leaking to the public without your knowledge because of the various passwords that you can use within the program.

Issues with Password Protection in Excel

The problem with Excel passwords is that it can be easily removed. Excel passwords are not encrypted, so it is easy for users to crack them if they have the motivation to do so. The only password that offers added protection is one created for workbook protection. In addition to the password you create as author of the spreadsheet, there is a master password that is required before you access the document. However, it is a publicly known master password, which is why it does not add extra protection for the Excel spreadsheet.

Only the encrypted password that you can create for Excel would be the one for opening the documents itself. However, the strength of the encryption entirely depends on the version of the program that you are using. This condition means that the older version you have, the weaker the encryption.

To solve this problem, it would help you to be aware of the program version that you are using right now. By doing this, you will be able to increase your security measures accordingly. Purchase the latest version of Excel if you can afford it. It would also help you to choose characters that are not commonly used for your password.

For example, you can combine the numbers and letters as well as symbols when trying to figure out which password to use. This will increase the security of your encryption significantly.

This concludes the very basics you simply *need* to know to proceed any further.

Chapter 2: Functions and Formulas

Perhaps the most important feature of Excel (and its strongest), functions and formulas are something you will have to use in order to make significant progress with your spreadsheet. A formula is just a mathematical expression, which calculates the value present of a cell. Functions are just the predefined formulas that Excel has already compiled for your use.

Let's make use of a formula for better understanding. Perform the following and observer what happens:

- Select any cell, say B4.
- Enter some value in B4.
- Do the same with another cell, B5.
- Suppose you want add these two. In cell B6, first type the '=' sign. This sign tells Excel that it should get ready to display the result of a calculation you're going to perform.
- Now you can either type "=B4+B5" or just select the first cell, add the mathematical sign, and select the second cell.
- Hit enter, and watch the sum of the 2 numbers get displayed in the cell B6.

That is pretty much it! Formulas are so simple to use, and also extremely powerful. You can edit a formula whenever and however you want. Simply click the cell where the formula was typed, then change the details on the **Formula**

bar above. The changes will be reflected immediately.

Unfortunately, formulas have to be typed out. This means that when you want to add or subtract about 15 to 20 different cells, you're going to have to add the + sign every single time. This is where **Functions** come in. They are predefined, they are easy to use, and they are designed for quick operations. For better understanding on using a function to your advantage, do the following example:

- Select a cell, say A8.
- Click on the **FX** button near the **Formula bar**. This is the **Insert Function** button.
- In the **Insert Function** dialog box, the functions are grouped into categories so that you can choose the required function with ease. Select the function you want and click OK.
- In the **Range** box, select the range of cells you want to perform the function on.
- Finally, select OK.

The function you've entered will be performed and the results will be displayed. Try experimenting with different functions to see what each one does, so that you familiarize yourself with them.

Repeatedly throughout this section, it has been mentioned that functions and formulas are very powerful. If calculation were the only thing they could perform, they would not be all that powerful, would they? No, what makes them powerful is that they are dynamic. Usually, when a result is displayed, you would expect the value of the result alone to get stored in the cell. This is not true. Excel uses the cell reference to perform calculations, not the actual numbers. In essence, what this means is that when you change the value of a particular cell, the change **will** be reflected in all the cells that have some sort of a relation with the first cell. For example:

- Type in some random values, say 5, 6, 7, 8, in 4 different, adjacent cells.
- In the very next cell, use a **Sum** function to add these 4 cells.
- Observe the result 26, and make note of it.
- Change the value of any one of the cells. Let us make a change from 8 to 10.

If Excel's formulas and functions weren't dynamic, the result 26 should have remained as it is. But it now changes to 28. That's where the power lies. All you need is a formula, and any changes you make will be taken in account while the formula is evaluated. This makes creating tables easier, but also editing them. You do not really need to keep track of which cell content is used where with the help of Excel Functions and Formulas.

Let us now take a look at some of Excel's functions:

Sum and Sumif

The most popular function, the **sum** function simply adds the range of cells you have given and displays the results. Of course, any changes made to these cells will reflect on the sum. The general syntax of the Sum function is given by:

=SUM(x:y)

Here, x and y are cells, and all the cells between x and y will be selected, and the contents added. You can simply type out these cell references, or just select them with your mouse. An example for adding 2 numbers using formula was given above. Try the same with the function to get the feel of how the Sum function works.

The sumif function works the same way, but it needs a condition. It's a condition that must be satisfied by the contents of the cell for them to be added. The syntax for sumif is:

=SUMIF(x:y,"condition1", "condition2")

Just replace "condition" by whatever you need. There doesn't necessarily have to be two conditions. There can be any number of conditions as required. It is sort of like a C program's if statement. For example:

- Type values in C1 to C5.
- In C6, use the **sumif** function, and select the range C1:C5.
- In the condition, give **>5**.
- You will now observe that in cell C6, only those numbers that are greater than 5 in C1:C5 have been added.

The sumif function is the ideal choice when you're doing a statistics report and you need to add up values that go beyond a certain range.

Count and Countif

Used when you need to know the number of cells in a particular column or row. An extension to this is the countif, where a condition is specified for the numbers. Only if the condition is satisfied will the cell be counted. The syntax of count and countif is given by:

=COUNT(x:y)
=COUNTIF(x:y,"condition1", "condition2")

Replace the condition by whatever condition you need.

Let us take an example for better understanding:

- Type in values from A1 to A5.
- In A6, add the **Count** function and select the range A1:A5.
- You will notice the number 5. This means that there are 5 cells in the range you have selected.

- Do the same, but add a condition that the number should be greater than 5.
- Do this by giving **>5** within the quotes.

This will display a certain value, which is the number of cells that contain a number greater than 5. This function is extremely useful when you need to quickly find out how many entries have been made that is greater than or less than a particular value.

Cell References

There are 3 types of cell references in Excel. They can get quite confusing, so there are some examples illustrated to point out the differences between each of the references clearly. The three reference types are:

➢ Relative
➢ Absolute
➢ Mixed

Before jumping straight into the 3 references, let's discuss a bit about what reference actually means. References are the names of cells, put simply. Each cell is addressed by its reference, and not by anything. This has a major advantage! Consider a cell having a mathematical formula that relates cell B2 and B3. If the contents of B2 and B3 are changes, so does the cell containing the formula. The changes made *will* be reflected.

With that short introduction, let us take a look at each of the references along with examples:

Relative Reference

Excel uses this reference type by default. When you click on a cell that contains a formula which looks something like "**=A1*B1**", then it is called a relative reference. It's called relative because, if the cell containing the formula is dragged somewhere, then the cell references automatically adjust themselves. That is, they don't stay as A1 and B1 anymore, but now they become A2 and B2.

Let us try to understand what relative reference means with a clear example:

- Enter some data in the range A1:A5.
- Do the same in the range B1:B5.
- In cell C1, type a formula that relates A1 and B1. It can be anything, but for simplicity, let us assume addition being carried out, that is, **=A1+B1**.
- Now select cell C1, and drag the cell (by clicking and holding the bottom right corner of the cell) up to cell C5.
- Now it is time to observe. Note that here; the cell C1 references the two cells to its left.

What you typed in was only A1+B1. But since it is in relative reference, when the same formula is applied in cell C2, it changes to A2+B2. Similarly in cells C3, C4, and C5, it becomes A3+B3, A4+B4, A5+B5 respectively. Notice how Excel adjusts the references the two cells tot he left by itself? Naturally, this also means that any changes made in any of the specified cells will be reflected accordingly. There are no exceptions to this in relative reference. This comes in handy when you're dealing with a large amount of data that needs to apply in a mathematical equation, and each set of data should have the same equation. Simply create the equation in one particular cell. Drag it down or to the right, and watch the intelligent Excel do your work for you!

Absolute Reference

If you need to have a certain set of data applied in a mathematical equation along with a constant value, then absolute reference is the way to go. For example, consider the conversion dollars to pounds. A logical way of conversion would be to enter the amounts of dollars in a particular column, and use a formula "=**A1*x**" where x would be the conversion factor. Though logical, it has a certain flaw. You will have to click on the cell, and make the conversion changes yourself every time the dollar to pound conversion factor changes. The easiest way to do it would be by giving an absolute reference.

Unlike in relative reference, where the relative cells vary as the formula is dragged down, an absolute reference to a cell means that that particular cell will be used throughout the cells in which the formula has been applied. The general syntax to create an absolute reference to a cell is:

$column$row (for example, B3)

The $ sign indicates the particular column or row to be constant. If you want the row to be constant, leave out the first $ sign. Similarly, if the column is desired to be constant, leave out the second $ sign.

Let us take an example:

- Type in some dollar values in the cell range A1:A5
- In cell E1, type in the conversion factor to convert dollars to pounds (let's consider this as 'x' here for simplicity).
- Now in cell B1, type in "**=A1*E1**".
- Click on B1, and drag it down using the drag option in the bottom right corner of the cell.
- Now observe each cell and its formula.

You can now see that all the cells take a relative reference to the cells in column A, but a fixed reference to the cell E1. Any change made in E1 will reflect in the cells of column B.

Mixed Reference

Mixed Reference is a combination of the Relative and

Absolute References. You usually will not be using mixed reference, unless your spreadsheet has formulas that connect different rows and columns at the same time. This is quite difficult to explain if you don't try it out yourself, so the entire concept has been illustrated with the help of an example. Make sure you try out the example as you read along in order to understand it better. The easiest example would be a multiplication table.

- Enter numbers 1 through 10 in in the cell range A2:A11.
- Enter numbers 1 through 10 in the cell range B1:K1.
- Now out goal is to create a multiplication table. Let us try using Relative and absolute references first.
- Enter the formula **=A2*B1** in the cell B2. Now drag it throughout the entire cell range.

You will notice that the numbers become quite huge. Now observe each of the cells and its formula. You will notice that since relative reference is used, the cells start multiplying the numbers directly above them and directly to the left of them. Thus the extremely huge values.

Now enter the formula **=A2 * B1** in cell B2. Now drag the formula throughout the entire cell range. You will notice that the entire range displays 1. This is because the reference, being absolute, ends up multiplying only cells A2 and B1 in all the cells.

This is where you may face problems. If you can't use relative and absolute references, then what can you use? That's where mixed reference comes in. You basically want the row to be constant in one multiplication term, and the column to be constant in the other. Therefore, what this is means is that the first term has a relative reference to the column, and the second term has a relative reference to the row. Let us try this out now in our multiplication table.

Enter the same data as before.
Now in cell B2, type the following formula: **=B\$1*\$A2**.
Drag this formula throughout, and you will notice the right values appearing in your table!

Let us analyze what we have done here. In the first term B\$1, we have created an absolute reference to the row, but a relative reference to the column. In the second term, the opposite is done. Now in cell B3, observe the formula. It should say **B\$1*\$A3**. Notice how only the row of column A has changed? Similarly, each of the cells in the range will have the right cells in the formula because of the mixed reference. Your multiplication table is now complete, along with your understanding of mixed reference!

Text

Excel isn't always about numbers. It has got functions that can manipulate strings to the maximum as required. There are several text functions, and a few important ones are discussed below with examples:

Join Strings

If you have C or C++ coding knowledge, then this is the Excel counterpart to string concatenation. In other words, it's just joining 2 strings together. The added benefit here, though, is that you can add a space whenever you want, wherever you want. The general syntax is:

=A1&B1

Use the ampersand symbols (&) whenever different cells or spaces are to be included. To include spaces, simply use: " " (a space within double quotes). Note that you have to add the ampersand symbol for even the spaces, so a cell that needs to join strings from A1 and A2 with a space in between would look like this:

=A1&" "&B1

Extracting strings

You get a part of a string as well. You can extract a string either from the left, right, or the middle.

Left: The general syntax is: **=LEFT(A1,x)** where x is the

number of letters you would like to extract. Spaces are included as a character as well, so be careful.

Right: The general syntax is: =**RIGHT(A1,x)**, where x is the number of letters. Spaces are included as characters.

Mid: The general syntax is: =**MID(A1,x,y)** where the letters extracted start from x in A1 and end at y in A1. Once again, spaces are included.

Len

This is used to get the length of a string. Unfortunately, this also includes spaces, so if the cell contains more than 1 string, an additional number will be added. The general syntax is:

=**LEN(A1)**

Logical Functions

Logical functions work with only 2 values, namely TRUE and FALSE. All the logical functions have certain conditions that may or may not be satisfied. If the conditions are satisfied, the result is taken to be TRUE, and the corresponding action is carried out. If the condition fails then the result is taken to be FALSE.

There are 3 logical functions in Excel:

➢ If
➢ And

➢ Or

IF

This statement is used to check a condition, and based on whether the condition is satisfied or not, one of two possible actions is carried out. The general syntax is:

=IF(condition,action1, action2) where action1 is the action for TRUE, and action2 for FALSE.

Let us take an example, where cell C3 must display the larger of the values stored in cells C1 and C2.

➢ Enter value 10 in C1.
➢ Enter value 25 in C2.
➢ Now in cell C3, type in the formula: **=IF(C1>C2, C1, C2)**

Observe that 25 gets displayed. What Excel does here is, it first checks the values stored in cells C1 and C2. If C1 happens to be greater, then C1 is displayed in C3. Else, C2 is displayed in C3. You are not limited to just displaying the numbers as such. You can perform any mathematical operation of the numbers. For example, =IF(C1>C2, C1/5, C2*10) would still give you the correct results. You are also not constrained to using just numbers. You can add text in the actions argument by placing them within double quotes as show below:

=IF(C1>C2, "C1 is greater", "C2 is greater")

The IFERROR

On the other hand, the IFERROR formula is the direct opposite of the previous one. This change will allow you to make cells yield results that correspond to the errors in the table. The syntax for this formula would look something like this:

Syntax: =IFERROR(VALUE A)OPERATION(VALUE B)"TRUE","FALSE"

As an example, let us go back to the grading table to record test scores that "you" were making for your students. Let us say that one of your students was not able to complete the requirements needed to pass your subject; then you would have to fill in their cells with incomplete. You can translate this into an IFERROR formula by using this syntax.

Syntax: =IFERRORA1=0="INCOMPLETE"

This action will enter the word incomplete onto the next column or cell with "0" as its value. Always remember to put in "=" before each formula. Otherwise, the syntax will be rendered erroneous, and you will not be able to yield the results that you would like to achieve.

AND

The AND function is used when you want a particular action to be performed if and *only if* all the conditions are TRUE. If any one of the conditions become FALSE, the action for the FALSE statement is carried out. The syntax for the AND statement is as follows:

AND(condition1, condition2)

Note that the AND function cannot be used alone since it returns only a TRUE or FALSE. Let us take an example using an IF statement, where the condition of the IF statement is carried out with the help of the AND function. You are also not limited to just 2 conditions. You can use as many conditions as you want, just make sure to separate each condition with a comma.

➢ Enter a value in A1.
➢ Enter a value in B1.
➢ In   cell   C1,   type   the   following:
    =IF(AND(A1>20,A2<5),"True part","False part").

Depending on the values given in A1 and B1, either "True part" or "False part" appears in cell C1.

OR

The OR function is used when you want a particular action to be performed if *any* of the given conditions turn out to be TRUE. If you want all the conditions to be true before an action is carried out, then it's best you use the AND function. Commonly made mistakes include switching out the OR and AND functions whenever it's needed, so be careful. The general syntax of the OR function is as follows:

OR(condition1, condition2)

As with the AND function, you cannot use OR alone since it just returns a TRUE or FALSE value. Similarly, you can add as many conditions as you wish, each condition separated by a comma.

Let us take an example to understand how the OR function works:

> ➤ Enter a number in A1.
> ➤ Enter a number in A2.
> ➤ In cell A3, type the following formula: **=IF(OR(A1>0,A2>0),"At least one positive","All negative")**.

If the numbers in A1 and A2 are negative, only then does the second condition, that is, "all negative" statement gets displayed. If either of them is positive, or if both are positive, then the first condition is executed.

OR and AND functions can use multiple conditions. However, the maximum limit of the number of conditions is 255. This is, however more than sufficient since you really shouldn't be using more than 5-10 conditions in one statement.

Differences and Problematic Areas in Excel

Previous versions of Excel were limited to the number of cells per workbook, with a limit of around 64,000 cells. Since 2007, the number has increased to a massive one million. Understandably, there are many issues you may expect when it comes to managing data through Excel, especially in the area of data analysis. This section will discuss those limitations in detail.

According to research, there are four general problematic areas for Excel when it comes to data analysis. These are as follows:

- Values, especially in large quantities tend to be mishandled. Some go missing; others are misrepresented therefore resulting to inconsistent byproducts and mathematical computations.

- Depending on the necessary analysis, data organization will differ substantially. This event will force any user to organize the data manually to accommodate different types of analytic systems.

- Data analysis can only be done for one column at a time. This problem makes the work slow and tedious to do because you would have to do the same computations again repeatedly for every column.

- Output tends to be organized poorly. There is an inadequate labeling system and the estimates for the yielded values in the table remain unseen. Because of this, whenever you use Excel, you won't be able to explain in detail how you got the computations. If you wanted to do this, you would have to record your calculations manually.

Because of these findings, Excel should be considered useful in terms of data entry and data preparation for statistical analysis. However, once you have prepared your data it is recommended that you use another program for calculating the statistics. Statistical calculation packages such as Stata, Minitab or Sys-tab are particularly useful. This way, you will not have difficulty getting reliable results as soon as possible.

Misconceptions about Excel

Like any other program, there are bound to be misconceptions about Microsoft Excel. This section will deal with the myths and the reality behind them.

1. The Need for Charts

The first myth is that you always have to have a chart to correspond with your data or for every presentation you make using Excel. This is not true. Sometimes all you need to express the results of your calculations is a statistical computation. It is that simple!

2. You Should Master Technology to Use Excel Well

The idea that you have to be a super user or a computer nerd to really master Excel is another misconception. While learning more about Excel is important, it is not the end all and be all of your business. Yes, Excel will help you make charts and graphs, but you also have to understand what those charts and graphs are about before you can use them effectively. Therefore, if I were you, I would learn more about the business in addition to Excel.

3. Always Rely On Defaults

Sometimes because of time constraints, we tend to stick to something we know rather than using a new method. This also applies to the use of Excel, especially when it comes to charts or graphs. However, a professional Excel user knows that an efficient table is one that is tailor-made to a particular data set. Besides, if you try to use defaults to present the large numbers of your data especially in an Excel 2003, you will end up failing for sure.

4. The Vendors Always Use the Best Templates

Just because you can get a few high-tech tools or templates from Excel vendors, doesn't mean you have to use them or that they are the best option. You have to be able to pick the best templates out from the crowd and use them to make your data truly stand out. Always check the Excel templates or preview them before you purchase.

5. The More Colorful That Chart Is The Better The Presentation

This concept is not necessarily always the case. Sometimes, simplicity regarding presentation will lead an individual to success when it comes to business. It all depends on the audience and how receptive they are to your data. Sometimes, you have to think about how others will see the presentation of first before you even make it.

6. A Good Chart Always Has Values

While values and numbers are important in charts, it is not always good to have the complete set of values in one chart. Most of the time, labels and values can only serve to distract the audience from the actual heart of the matter. It would be best to keep it short when trying to label your charts. Also, do not bombard your audience with numbers if they are not necessary. Always be creative in your presentation.

7. A Good Chart Should Always Be Quick To Read

This belief is not always true. It does not matter if your chart is complicated or simple. What is important is that you can share the information efficiently and that the information you want to come across is presented well. If you want your peers to know something about your data and values, don't hesitate to explain that when necessary.

The most important thing to remember when making an Excel chart is that it should always contain pertinent information about the topic at hand. Efficiency is paramount when it comes to information sharing.

Summary

This chapter is just a short history on the evolution of Excel as a computer program. In the following paragraphs, you'll learn more about how Excel operates and what you can expect from the various versions of the program. We will also discuss some of the differences that can be found in each program and how they can work for you as an individual consumer.

Functions and formulas associated with Excel will also be examined. You will also learn how you can use it to make your academic life even easier. Additionally, you will also learn about the different shortcuts that you can use to operate and navigate the program.

Additional Functions of the Program

Aside from data entry, Excel is also perfect for simple calculations, including averages and standard deviations. There are commands and formulas you can utilize to get results for single entries or a range of entries in any given worksheet. This ability is what makes Microsoft Excel a truly dynamic computer program.

Moreover, Excel has the ability to link or communicate with other Windows applications within the Office suite of programs (Microsoft Word, Microsoft Access, etc.). This total connectivity enables the applications to exchange data and use each program's inherent capabilities to further manipulate data. This ability is formally known as **Dynamic Data Exchange** and it is commonly employed in various financial markets. For example, news organizations will use this protocol to exchange data with services like Reuters or Bloomberg.

Utilizing External Data

Excel can also make use of external data from other programs within the computer system. This action is done through various Microsoft Office connections using .odc connections within the MS Office data connection format.

You can also update the Excel files on your hard drive through utilizing an ODBC driver directly supplied by Microsoft. In addition, Excel can work with add-ins to allow communication with outside websites and data sources, for example, Power Plus Pro and the Productivity Suite.

For the more advanced Excel users, you can also utilize programs like Real Time Data. However, as mentioned earlier, it is not easy to understand and use because of the lack of proper documentation from supported data vendors.

The Spreadsheet Export and Migration

Certain APIs can help you open Excel spreadsheets using a variety of applications and computerized environments outside of Excel. You can open spreadsheets on the web using ActiveX controls or Flash players. Java can also help you navigate and write Excel spreadsheets without difficulty. Their other open source Matt programs that can help you migrate your spreadsheet without difficulty into other programs. Some of these open source programs are as follows:

- Apache POI

- Excel Package
- PHP Excel
- Excel Services

Some of these programs are even known to convert Excel files into readable objects for the web applications, especially in the latest version of the program. For this reason, you never have to worry about being able to open or read spreadsheets if you do not have access to Microsoft Excel.

Printing Documents

There are many other programs that you can use to write Excel spreadsheets. One example is the Microsoft Excel Viewer. It is free and similar to Microsoft Word when it comes to functionality. Unfortunately, though, this program does not have an updated version for Mac.

These are just some of the many issues regarding the functionality and security of Microsoft Excel. Like any computer program, go to next cell is Excel has weaknesses and strengths. These idiosyncrasies are why you have to use the program in conjunction with other Microsoft Office tools to get the most out of it. This way, you will be able to find out which areas you can use Excel for and which areas to compensate before it is too late.

Excel Tips and Tricks: Other Surprises You Can Expect from the Program

Whether you are an Excel expert or not, this will be a good program to use whenever you need to create various charts and graphs professionally or as a hobby. This section will give you some ideas as to what else you can do with the program aside from those already mentioned. We will also give you some ideas as to what you can do with Excel in connection with other Microsoft Office programs on your computer.

Preliminary Reminders

The following tips and tricks apply to Microsoft Excel 2010. In the next few chapters, we will deal with the latest versions of Excel and the commands that harness the program's capabilities without difficulty.

The One Click Button to Select

First, you must figure out what version of Excel you are using. The 2010 version will have a "one click to select" button that enables you to select multiple cells with a single click. It certainly will make you work much faster than you normally would.

Opening Excel Files in Bulk

In addition to this, you also have the opportunity to open the files in bulk with Excel 2010. You can do this by selecting the data in the window and press the enter key on the keyboard.

Shifting between Different Excel Files

Another trick is shifting between Excel files. This can be useful if you have different worksheets open at one time. Since it can be confusing to work between the two sheets,

Excel 2010 has the ability to navigate sheets quickly through dressing Ctrl + Tab. This allows the user to "tab" through the Excel worksheets easily. This command is also applicable for other Windows 7 programs Like Word or PowerPoint.

Creating New Shortcuts

You can also create new shortcuts using Excel 2010. Normally, there are just three alternatives that can be found in the topmost menu, they are: Undo, Redo, and Save. However, if you want to unlock your shortcuts, here are some commands that you should follow.

Click File-Open-Quick Access Toolbar. From there, you can add more commands just like Cut and Copy. After this, you can save it. You should see the additional commands at the top of the menu.

Adding Lines within Cells

If you would like to add a diagonal line across a cell, click More Borders. By doing this, you will be able to get more features. These functions include a Diagonal Line. Remember after modifying your cell, always save your changes.

Navigation and Copying Data

On the other hand, if you want to move quickly through columns within the spreadsheet, select a cell you want to copy from then move the cursor to the borders and wait until the cursor changes to a cross arrow icon. After this, you can drag and move the column freely.

But what if you want to copy data from other cells? Simply press the Ctrl button and then drag. The new column will copy data from the cell you have dragged, it is that easy.

Search: Speedy, Wild Card and Vague

You can also search your cells faster by activating the speedy search feature. You can do this by typing Ctrl and F simultaneously. This way, you will not spend hours of your day trying to find a single cell value in a spreadsheet. It will certainly save you time and energy for sure.

The Ctrl+F shortcut is good if you know the exact values or parameters of what you're trying to find. However, if you are not sure of the specifics, you will have to use what's called a Wild Card feature.

In Excel 2010, you can perform a vague search of a spreadsheet by typing either "?" or "*". The question mark will have you find a single character at a time while the asterisk will help find combinations of characters in the spreadsheet.

Supplementary Conditions

There is another condition that you have to keep in mind when using these two wildcard characters. You would have to make sure that you type in a wave line in front (~) for the command to be recognized as a target result.

Generating Unique Values

In addition to this, you can also create unique values within a column by using the advanced filter feature. You would need to do this often if you need to extract a single value from either the data cell or the column.

Unique values can be created with the following commands:

Click the column that you want to work on, then go to Data—Advanced. Once that window pops up, click the command Copy to Another Location. Once you have clicked this, you have to specify the target location by typing the cell value or clicking the cell where you want the data to transfer (area-choosing).

For example, if you want to find a certain age from the list in your worksheet. Let's say the age is in Column C but you want to have the value also shown in Column E, then you'll select Unique Records and click OK. However, there may be differences in the value within the current column vs. the original data so you may want to copy the data to another location to prevent any discrepancies.

An Excel worksheet can also be used to validate your data. To do this, you have to define some restrictions regarding the values to be encoded into the spreadsheet. For example, if you are trying to correlate age with the number of participants in your survey, you have to put in some parameters regarding the specific values that you can encode into the spreadsheet. In this case, let us say that the participants are all females ranging from 25 to 60 years old. To ensure that there would be a limit to how much content is encoded, it would help to define the parameters according to the age of the participants.

Specific Commands: Setting the Parameters

With Input Restriction, there are certain commands that you need to follow. In this case, since you are trying to restrict the age limit within the spreadsheet, you would have to go to data—data validation—setting. After this, you have to type in the new parameters you want to set. For example, if you want to limit the participants in age from 25 to 60, you should set the parameters accordingly.

Subsequently, you will receive a prompt that will require you to set up input messages. By doing this, the participants will then receive automatic reminders that will tell them about the restrictions. In this case, they may receive messages similar to this one. "Please type in your age now"

You can include specific directions as well, such as the age range and the type of number itself, (whole number). Users who do not adhere to these guidelines will get a warning message about the wrongly encoded data and will be asked to try again.

The Rundown

These are just a few of the major tips that you can use when working with Excel. These tricks are just one way to maximize how Excel performs as a program. The key is to be aware of the commands, what they are and how to use them. Once you learn this, it will be easy to find the right data and then classify it into a useful set.

Added Information

This section will discuss some additional shortcuts in Excel navigation. These shortcuts are designed to make your workflow a little easier. You will have the opportunity to learn more about these commands and also the steps needed to execute them without difficulty. Before we go further, though, here is a list of the significant keys that will be used in the navigation of the Excel program.

- Ctrl
- Alt
- Del

These are known as individual keys. When used in conjunction with other characters on the keyboard they allow the user to perform certain actions that will affect the open program. Sometimes these actions are referred to as "keyboard shortcuts". For the purpose of this explanation, using keyboard shortcuts within an Excel worksheet will allow the user to perform actions quicker. These actions include the transposition of data, copying, deleting and many others. The tips and tricks above make use of these commands often so learning these commands is essential to become an expert in Excel.

Fast Navigation

When it comes to navigation within a worksheet, all you have to do is to press the Ctrl button and arrow keys simultaneously. This action will allow you to move the cursor to the edge of the worksheet. You can move the cursor in different directions as well. The Ctrl button, plus the use of the arrow keys is a great way to navigate around your data within a worksheet.

Special Tasks that could be performed in Excel

With Excel, a user will be able to carry out compartmentalized tasks that will make the manipulation of data easier than ever. In addition to data manipulation, gathering results will also be more streamlined. Some of the examples of data manipulation and results gathering include transposition, hiding and data composition.

Steps on How to Transpose Data via Excel

Transposing data is one way you can manipulate your data set. This can be accomplished through a keyboard shortcut and we are going to walk through the steps below:

- First, you have to highlight the area that you want to transpose.
- Once the area is highlighted, right-click and select copy.
- Then, place the cursor into any blank cell or column where you want the data to transfer.
- Afterward, you can highlight the empty cell and go to Home-Paste and Transpose.

Always remember that the command will not be executed unless you can copy the necessary data first. Otherwise, you would have to repeat the whole process again.

Related Features

Hiding Important Data

With the Excel program in your arsenal, you will be able to hide critical data for security purposes. You can do this within the worksheet by pressing the following keys:

For Smaller Data Pieces

If you are going to hide only a few pieces of data, you have to right-click the cell or the range of cells that you would want to include, then click hide.

For Larger Groups of Data

On the other hand, if you would want to protect a large amount of data, you can do this by utilizing this particular format cell function. Here are some of the said commands that will activate this particularly computerized role for your benefit.

First, choose the data that you would want to hide and click select.

After this, you can go ahead and access:

- Home
- Choose font
- Open format cells
- Number tabs
- Custom
- Type

After following these commands, you can now click OK. Then, all of the values that you have typed in each cell will become invisible. It will only be seen in the **Preview Area** right next to the **Function** button.

Composing Text in One Cell

It may be difficult to produce some words and make them fit into one cell. However, with the use of special characters like the ampersand (&), you will be able to make a few characters appear within one cell. You can do this by following these simple steps.

First, choose a cell where you would want to utilize for the results.

Afterward, type in the cell designation numbers that can be found on the side of the worksheet in one line. For example, if you would want to have the words, Liza, USA and 25 appear in one cell, you will type in the following variables along with the ampersand in between:

A1&B2&C2

As a result, the characters LizaUSA25 will be issued in the next cell. The change will make it easier for you to type in multiple characters without having to expand the cell unnecessarily.

Unique Operations

How to Include Zero in the Cells

Do you want to include a character with a zero at the beginning? By default, Excel will delete zeros automatically. However, there's always a way around that. You can prevent the program from the leading zeros automatically by placing the number in quotation marks. This alteration will lead the program to recognize zero as a part of the character line being typed.

For example:

If you are going to type something like 0.21 in the cell, it would be best to represent this as "0".21.

The One Click and Double Click Features

You can usually use the one-click feature to get various unique values such as summations and averages. However, you can also use it to get more functions and statuses out of Excel. This is accomplished by moving the pointer to the bottom of the sheet and right clicking the tabs.

In addition to the one-click feature, you can also rename your worksheet by double clicking. Most people will just right click the cell with your file name and choose Rename. However, double clicking the cell will be much faster. By doing this, you will also be able to rename the document directly.

There are just a few of the many tips, tricks and shortcuts available to you in Excel. You should practice these because when you perfect them, it allows you to be more efficient and maximize your efforts. Knowing these simple steps will enable you to complete work in Excel even if you're under a deadline. Working with Excel doesn't have to be tedious, you just have to be willing to explore all the possible options and functions. Once you learn these shortcuts, you'll get an amazing amount of functionality back from Excel.

In the following chapters, you'll learn more about Excel shortcuts. We will also discuss the latest version of Microsoft Excel and look at what the future holds for the program.

Significant Formulas that Every Excel User Should Have

Just because you have mastered the basics of Excel, your education should not stop there. Here are some additional skills that you should learn to make the most of your Excel experience. The sooner you learn these, the easier it will become to use Excel.

1. V-lookup

This power tool should be in every Excel's user playbook, V-Lookup is a valuable way to locate scattered data throughout the worksheet. How does it accomplish this? V-Lookup classifies all of your data into a single pool, this makes it easier to find and retrieve. For example, V-Lookup can help you manage large lists, like a store inventory.

If you work in retail, there is a good chance that you will have to deal with an inventory sooner or later. Store inventories are ways that a business can record and classify items in their stock, usually with a corresponding serial number. The V-Lookup formula enables you to pull out a specific serial number from the entire list, then update or replace it within the system.

It works in such a way that it will match the serial number on the products with a recorded serial numbers on your inventory list.

Writing the Formula

When typing an Excel formula, it is important that you write the equal sign or "=" first before writing the command string itself. In this case, you will write the V-lookup formula on the formula bar just like how you see it below.

=VLOOKUP(

After this, you can write the items that you want to search for and put them inside the parentheses. In this case, let us say that you are looking for a tomato juice brand. The formula will then look something like this:

=VLOOKUP(Brand X...)

Now, you can move on to entering the cell and range number that contains the data. You have to type in the necessary information to retrieve the data. Here is an example:

=VLOOKUP(Brand X A1: B12)

It is crucial to remember that the program will tend to search for items in the first column of the spreadsheet. Therefore, you should write coordinates or the range that corresponds to the first items in your column lists. This way, you will not have any problems using the particular command in the long run.

The next step would be to add the column index number. This value will specify the corresponding column name that you are hoping to determine. For example, if you are looking for an item in the second column of your worksheet, the formula will look as follows:

=VLOOKUP(Brand X A1: B12, 2)

After this, you can also find approximate matches that could be on the list. To do this, you have to write either True or False. If you write the former, it will look for an approximate value closest to what you already typed. Otherwise, it will look for values that are not clearly similar to what you are obtaining.

Remember that this particular command looks for exact matches so most of the time it will work on base with exact numerical values given. It should look something like this one.

=VLOOKUP(Brand X A1: B12, 2, TRUE)

Now, you can press the enter key, and you will hopefully find the specific values that you are trying to find.

Pivot Tables

These automated tables would let you compute all other operations and calculations in Excel. For the 2013 version, this program added recommendations for Pivot Tables. The tables made it easier for users to create customized tables that will display the data that they needed.

Creating a Pivot Table

To help you create this particular type of table, you have to make sure that you have a single name for your data cluster. After this, you can go to the insert-pivot table. You can now add your data range upon seeing the window.

After this, you would be able to see your available fields at the top right-hand-side of the bar. The bottom half of them will be reserved for generating the tables that you would need.

Pivot Charts

A pivot chart is a powerful data analysis tool that can be used for a wide variety of reporting functions in Excel. These individual types of charts allow you to glance at complex data. It has a combination of traditional Excel table functions with various data series, categories and similar features. However, Excel 2013 made it more interactive by allowing you to explore the data subsets without difficulty.

This program also added the Recommended Pivot Charts feature. This element can be found under the Recommended Excel Charts feature within the INSERT TAB. This feature allows you create the chart on your own without difficulty.

Creating Charts

To create your table successfully, you have to enter your data into the Excel worksheet with various column headers. After this, you can do the following commands.

- Insert
- Chart
- Chart Type

As soon as you are done creating your table, you will be able to use it for your presentations without delay. Excel even has a recommended table and maps feature, which will be discussed further in the book.

Transposing Columns and Rows

This skill will be useful if you are going to work with data that is presented in rows when you want them in columns or vice versa. You can do the transposition by just copying the row or column that you want to transpose. After this, you can right click on the cell location that you want to go to and select Paste Special. There will be the checkbox to appear at the bottom of the popup window named Transpose. Click OK and the rest will be history.

Summary

These features are helpful if you want to increase your efficiency working in Excel. This will enable you to generate faster results in large data sets in a very short amount of time. If you an exceptionally large quantity of data, it will help you process it that much quicker.

Bonus Features

1. Flash-Fill

This additional feature is one of the newest features in Excel 2013. It works in such a way that it can resolve one of the most severe problems that Excel users can face on a daily basis: retrieving pieces of combined data from a lone cell.

For example, if you are working on a column of the first and last names of your students, previously, you had to either type both characters manually. Alternatively, you would have to work with an incredibly complicated workaround that would usually take too much time.

With a flash-fill feature in Excel 2013, you will be able to add data with the formatting intact without using any formulas. If going back to the example of your students' names, you can just type the first names of the person that you would want to grade in the field and click on the following commands:

HOME- FILL - FLASH FILL

After entering this command, the program will be able to extract all the first names of the people on the list without difficulty.

Interested in other bonus features that will make Excel more productive? Check out the options below and you'll be an Excel expert in no time.

2. Quick Analysis

Quick Analysis helps simplify the creating of charts with a minimal data set. This means that you don't have to have all the information entered into a worksheet to generate a chart, Quick Analysis will take what you have and extrapolate from there.

The Quick Analysis feature comes with an interactive menu that allows formatting along with chart-creation and other useful features that will make your presentations even more attractive.

3. Creating Reports

If you want to create your reports using an Excel worksheet, you can do this by utilizing the Power View element. This component works in such a way that it lets you see massive amounts of data in one Excel worksheet without difficulty.

It even has a full-screen feature that will allow you to see the table completely without limitations. This enhancement will also enable you to export your table and additional data from Excel to PowerPoint, which will make for a more dynamic presentation of the report.

Activate this feature by going into Insert and clicking **Reports** in Excel 2013.

This concludes the chapter on some of the most basic and important functions and formulas that Excel offers you.

Chapter 3: MS Excel 2016

Most of the 2013 Excel features are present in the 2016 version. There are very few variations with the toolbars. All the functions and formulas presented to you in this book can be used in the 2016 version as well, without any problems. The group layout is slightly different in the **Data tab** and **Review tab**, but most of the other tabs are pretty much the same, with the same commands and functions.

One additional feature of the 2016 is the **Start Inking** present in the **Review** tab. This feature is slightly like the MS Paint software. You can add lines and curves. You can customize the thickness and the color. You also get the **Highlighter**, which you have to manually drag around to highlight anything of importance. With the **Eraser**, you can delete any of the curves or highlights you have made. These will not be discussed in detail since they are pretty self-explanatory.

Other Significant Improvements in Microsoft Excel 2016

Microsoft Excel 2016 has many other important enhancements that you will surely enjoy as the program user. This section will focus on giving you some ideas as to what you can expect from the latest version of Excel so you can be prepared when you finally update your program.

Merging

Some of the old add-ons from previous versions of Excel will give you increased performance and high-quality results without difficulty. Here are some of the add-ons that you will be able to experience with this particular upgrade.

- Power Queries
- Data Models
- One-Click Forecasting
- Power BI

With this high-tech program, you will also be able to create more tables and charts with just one click. You will also be able to share interactive reports with your co-workers when necessary.

Quick Analysis Tools

Quick Analysis Tools is an upgraded version of the previous shortcuts and quick access features found in prior versions of Excel.

A group of smart analysis tools will give you the opportunity to save time and effort when it comes to calculating the variables in your table. Once you have completed all the variables in your table, there is a lightning icon that you would be able to use to activate all the options available for manipulating the elements in the table.

Each button has a submenu that even has more options that will allow you to navigate the worksheets without difficulty.

Recommended Charts

Microsoft Excel 2016 has the recommended charts feature that will allow the user to create and format different tables automatically with various styles to be presented during meetings or symposiums. You can access this feature through the following commands.

- Highlight the database table
- Select Insert
- After this, you can go to recommended charts and choose from one of the available samples.

However, if you do not want to use the recommended charts, you can go to the All Charts tab and choose among the various categories on the list. Here are some of the categories that you can look forward to in the All Charts Tab.

Pareto – it will classify the bars from the highest first. This command, in turn, will show which of the bars have a bigger impact or the most significant increase. Use these various pieces of data to find out where you can assign your sources.

Waterfall –This is also known as a brick chart because it will show your data in such a way that the bars on the tables seem to hover over the worksheet giving it a three-dimensional look. This particular design will allow you to have a more interactive presentation in the future. It will seem like a cascading waterfall. Having been designed this way is why it is known as the waterfall chart.

New Templates Feature

The new template feature will allow you to view and use different samples of the Excel sheets that will be useful for presentations. It will also show you some tutorials on how to navigate the spreadsheet and make your own in the future.

The Power Maps

In Excel 2016, you can use mapping tools that will make it easier for you to create various charts and maps with three-dimensional images. With this feature, you will also be able to compare different amounts of data like temperature, or the amount of rainfall and population in one area depending on what you are looking for as a result.

Activating Auto Correct

Did you know that you can use auto correct functions in Excel? Yes, this feature is not only limited to Microsoft Word. You can activate this feature in Excel by going to file, options and proofing. Then you can enable the auto correct options and input to correct text into the Replace text box. This way, you would not have to correct every single word that you type manually. Excel will do it for you immediately. This feature is also included in the latest version of Excel, which will be discussed later in the book.

Tell me

The first thing you are definitely bound to notice when you start using Excel 2016 for the first time, the **Tell me** text box is your basic tour guide. You tell what you need, and it fetches or does it for you. For example, suppose you want to create a funnel chart. Just type in "**funnel**" and the Tell Me text box will pop up the option to create a funnel chart. You can type in anything you want, and a Smart Lookup will be performed on the terms you have entered. A really powerful tool to have, but it takes time to get used to. And when you do get used to it, it makes navigating around Excel so much easier and faster.

This setting is located on the right side of the ribbon menu after the final tab. It is useful if you want to perform short-term commands. The function is activated by clicking on the box, then waiting for the drop down menu to appear. Then, pick the item in the menu that applies to your task.

You will also be able to view the recent queries and issues that were solved using this particular feature. Then, you can also access a multitude of help menus to make the navigation even easier. You will also be granted internet access to find more substantial answers if you have any additional questions.

Autocomplete

The autocomplete feature is extremely useful and new in MS Excel 2016. You will not always be able to remember the entire function. Previously, this posed a serious problem, since you had to manually check the function from fx, which was a waste of valuable time. But with autocomplete, just typing in the first few letters that you do remember will bring up a list of functions that include the letters, and you can select from the list.

Funnel Charts

This type of chart is new and looks amazing. If you have details that require to be compared with a reference value, then using funnel charts would be best. Give the details of the reference first, and the very first value of your funnel chart will be the reference. The following will make the chart look like a funnel, and hence the name. The funnel shape also makes it easier to compare different values with the reference.

To create a funnel chart, do the following:

> ➢ Select the range of cells that contain the data.
> ➢ Click on **Insert tab.**
> ➢ Now click on **Insert Waterfall icon -> Funnel.**

Get & Transform

This is a new feature added to Excel 2016, that makes integrating databases into your spreadsheet much more simpler and quicker. Present in the **Data tab**, the **Get & Transform** group consists of commands that allow you to get and transform data, as well as perform complex calculations on them with relative ease. Previously, these features were possible only with a separate add-in, called the **Power Query**.

To add a new query, simply click on **Data tab**, then under the **Get & Transform** group, click on **Show queries**. From the given list, select either the file, or the database, or other sources, as necessary to include the query.

Sharing

Perhaps the strongest feature of all the software in Office 2016, your spreadsheet can now be shared and published. Click on the **Share** button in the Ribbon. You can share your spreadsheet via SharePoint, OneDrive and OneDrive for Business. Also, when files are stored in OneDrive for Business or SharePoint, you can also check the history to see what changes have been made by you or others who have permission to change the details, and also access the earlier versions. You can do this by going to **File -> History**.

Insights

Type a phrase, then **Right click -> Smart Lookup**, to open up the Insights Pane. Powered by the powerful search engine Bing, Insights will give your definitions and related Wikipedia pages. If you want to use the Smart Lookup without typing anything in your spreadsheet, head to **Review -> Smart Lookup** and type what you want there for the same results.

Ink Equations

Ever felt that typing out complex equations was tiresome and tedious? Well then, this feature should get your spirits up if you do not like equations all that much. In the **Symbols** group in the **Insert tab**, click on **Equation -> Ink Equation**. This should pop a window, where you can *write* the equation, and have it appear on the preview. Excel automatically converts your text into the corresponding equation, and writing equations has never before been easier! Though this feature was designed specifically for devices having a touch-screen, you can still use it with a desktop and a mouse.

Chapter 4: Shortcuts

No matter which software you are using, shortcuts play an important role. They save a lot of time that can spend productively on your actual content, instead of searching for the commands in each of the tabs. This chapter focuses solely on the most important shortcuts that you *have* to know in order to be quick with your Excel endeavors. These shortcuts are listed for both the Windows as well as OS X operating systems, respectively.

Create File

Ctrl + N
cmd + N

Open Workbook

Ctrl + O
cmd + O

With this shortcut, a window pops up, where you can select the workbook you want to work on. Note that the spreadsheet must already exist.

Save Workbook

Ctrl + S
cmd + S

Perhaps the most remembered shortcut, and most used, you are recommended to use this shortcut to occasionally save your workbook. You can never be sure that your spreadsheet will never crash. If you decide to not have AutoSave feature on, then this is the best option. Just hit Ctrl + S every time you take a break to save your file and save yourself the pain of performing the same actions all over again, in the unfortunate event of a crash.

Save As

F12
cmd+shift+S

Use this shortcut when you want to save the file with a different name.

Print File

Ctrl + P
cmd + P

When you need to take a print of a certain range of cells, then hitting this shortcut instead of the going to the tabs is the fastest way.

Close Workbook

Ctrl + F4
cmd + Q

Copy Cells

Ctrl + C
cmd + C

You can copy the selected range of cells using this shortcut. Copying cells also means that you copy their formula as well, so make sure you have your relative, absolute, and mixed references sorted out first before copying and pasting the cells elsewhere.

Cut Cells

Ctrl + X
cmd + X

Paste

Ctrl + V
cmd + V

The paste shortcut not only applies to the cells, but to anything that copied to the clipboard. This can be images, cells, charts, or even text and numbers.

Create Chart

F11
Fn + F11

Using this shortcut pops up the charts window, from where you can select the necessary charts.

These are some of the most basic shortcuts that you should know and use. Whenever you feel the need to perform any of these actions, make sure you perform the shortcut so you familiarize yourself with the keys. With practice, you can end up easily and quickly using these shortcuts instead of going through the ribbon. Make sure to learn these shortcuts. You should reach a state where your hands first go the shortcut before even thinking about moving to the options above.

When you are a beginner to MS Office in general, then all these shortcuts may overwhelm you. Be patient, come back and check this list occasionally to refresh your memory whenever you feel like it, and you should be able to grasp the shortcuts within a few hours. If you have used MS Word or Outlook or even PowerPoint, then these shortcuts should be a piece of cake to you, and you can apply them whenever you want.

Additional Keyboard Shortcuts

If you want to have easier navigation when it comes to your cells, you should know about some important keyboard shortcuts that will allow you to input formulas quickly. Some of these shortcuts will allow you to go through each cell without taking too much time.

Here is a list of other possible keyboard shortcuts that you can use in the latest versions of Excel.

- F2 – allows for editing of the cell using the formula bar.
- Control + Home – moves the cursor to the beginning of the worksheet
- Control + End –this will highlight the last cell in the worksheet
- Alt + = - this shortcut will automatically sum up the values directly above the chosen cell.
- Control + Down or Up Arrows - allows you to move to the top or bottom cell of the selected columns.
- Control + Left or Right Arrow - navigates all rows in the worksheet from left to right.

- Control or Shift + Down or Up Arrows – these keys allow the user to select the cell directly above or below the highlighted cell.
- Shift + F11 - this will enable you to create a blank worksheet within the same workbook or file.

These are just a few of the keyboard shortcuts that are useful when it comes to operating Excel. There are many more that you will learn as you use Excel too. However, for now, we'll focus on these and move on to other tips in the following chapters.

Chapter 5: Macros

Excel was intended to make your work easier. When it comes to repetitive tasks, there is no better solution than the Macro, which you can either create yourself, copy a macro or a part of the macro into another one, and then run it by clicking on the object that you are required to create as well.

The default Ribbon will not display the **Developer tab**, where the macro options are present. To solve this issue, go to **File -> Options**, then click on **Customize Ribbon**. Here, select the **Developer** checkbox under the **Main Tabs** list.

Now, in the **Developer tab**, click on **Record Macro**

- Enter a name for the macro. The name cannot be a cell reference.
- If you desire a shortcut for the macro, then just enter the shortcut you want in **Shortcut key** box.
- Store the macro wherever you want.
- Click on **OK**, to begin recording.
- Start doing whatever you feel is repetitive to store it in the macro.
- Once you are done, click on **Stop Recording** in the **Developer tabs**.

You have now successfully created a macro, which you can use whenever you want by either pressing the shortcut key or running it manually.

VBA

Excel Visual Basic for Applications or VBA in short, is the programming language that Excel uses. It is with the help of VBA that you create macros. VBA also has possibilities to avoid and mitigate the errors in macros.

Visual Basic: The Language of Excel

Microsoft Excel makes use of a unique programming language known as Visual Basic for Applications. This language works in such a way that it allows the user to program automatic tasks in Excel. These automated tasks are written into the program with the use of macros. In this particular section, we will further discuss how you can write your macro in a few simple steps.

To get started writing macros, you have to activate the developer mode in Excel. You can do this by going into the ribbon and customizing it. In the Excel spreadsheet, right click anywhere on the ribbon and click on "customize the ribbon". As soon as you click the customize ribbon tab, a menu window will pop up with a drop down list of the different modes that you can use with the program. Tick the "Developer Mode" box and you will be all set.

In developer mode, you will be able to set up additional commands for your spreadsheet to make your work even easier. You can do this by inserting additional control buttons into the spreadsheet itself. For example, by clicking add, you will discover the ActiveX controls. From those ActiveX controls, click on the command box. This window will serve as your message box for the particular macro spreadsheet. Upon the creation of the control or "commands" button, you can now drag it down to the worksheet itself.

In the following section, we will give you some of the essential functions of Microsoft Excel. We will also discuss the basics of file creation and how it can affect the function of the whole program.

Assigning Macros to objects

When you want a macro to be assigned to any object or graphic, you can do so by **Right clicking** the object. Then click on **Assign Macro**. In the **Macro Name** box, select whichever macro you need.

Now that you have a command button in the worksheet itself, you can proceed to design your macro into the spreadsheet. You can do this by right-clicking the command or control button. As soon as you do this, a drop-down menu will appear. You will be able to find a variety of commands listed. However, for this tutorial, click on "view code".

After this, the Visual Basic Editor will appear. Place the cursor in between the private sub-command button line and the English sub. Next, you ought to type in the range or cell name and value. The value refers to the characters that you would want to type in the cell.

Along with the command window, you will see another open window beside it. This dialog box is what you call the Project Explorer. Most of the time, it will appear in the Visual Basic Editor. However, if it does not show up the first time, you can select a project that you would want to work on, click view to see the window itself.

After this, you can successfully add the code line "Sheet 1" for the window to appear. After this, you will have created your very own macro for Microsoft Excel.

The Message Box

This particular feature mainly refers to the dialog box that you can use to tell various users that this specific event is occurring within the program. You can also type in different commands in this particular part of the sheet to navigate the window itself. For example, if you want to enter a value in any of the cells in the spreadsheet, you can just go to the message box and type in the cell number and the value that you want to enter. After typing it in, the particular value that you entered will appear in the cell instantly. This advantage is why the message box is considered as one of the most important features of an Excel spreadsheet.

The Object Hierarchy

In Excel, various larger characters can be contained within another cell or group of cells. This is what you call the **object hierarchy**. It can be very confusing to learn, but hopefully, this section will make it possible for you to understand and even use this particular part of Excel.

The Mother of All Objects

This particular statement applies itself to Excel. The Excel program is also known to have an application spreadsheet that you create. This element can be considered as a workbook object or file. In the worksheet, there can also be other kinds of objects such as the sheets or ranges.

In the previous section, we discussed how to create the macro spreadsheet and discussed how to build code. Always remember that if you want to make multiple codes, you have to separate them with a dot. This way, the computer will easily recognize what you are typing as code and subsequently be able to execute the command without any hassles.

It is also important to note that any mistake entered into the values put into the program will jeopardize the functionality of the entire system. This event is why you have to be very careful and concise about what you want to have the program do.

In addition, if you want to change any values are objects in the worksheet, you cannot do this by typing in commands in the message box. You would have to open the spreadsheet object accordingly.

Creating Collections

Collections or groups refer to a group of workbooks and worksheets clustered in one file. Think of it as one physical folder for every chart and document that you ever created for Excel. Creating collections will make it easier for you to organize the files in your Excel folder without difficulty.

The Range

This term refers to the number of cells that you have in your worksheet. These cells are where the significant values and variables of your chart are entered for computation. If you want to create a certain variable or formula in Excel, you have to enter it into each of the cells available.

For easier navigation, the program divided the cells into particular quadrants. If you look on top of your Excel sheet, you will see a series of numbers and letters on the upper left and top of the window. This set of characters corresponds to the number of cells as well as their position on the worksheet itself. For example, if you see a column of cells labeled A, chances are you'll also see tabs on the side of the window labeled A1, A2 and so forth.

This feature makes it easier to navigate through your worksheet especially if you have many values and variables to see. You can either move your arrow keys to scroll through the worksheet or just type the corresponding name of the cell on to the formula bar. After typing the proper commands, the cell that you are looking for will be highlighted, allowing you to continue your work without difficulty.

How to Deal With Macro Errors

If you experience errors in creating a macro, there are certain steps that you can take to correct this. This section will teach you how you can deal with macro errors effectively without affecting the right cells in your spreadsheet. Just follow these simple steps and it will be like nothing ever happened.

- First, place a command button on the worksheet. After this, you can add the following code lines:

  X = 2
  Range ("A1").Valu = X

- Click the command button on your sheet. If it yields a dialog box saying that there was a compile error and a variable is not found, you should click OK.
- The issue happened because the X variable was not defined in the code equation. You can solve this by declaring all your variables upon the creation of the system. This condition is what you call Option Explicit.
- After doing this, you should reset the visual basic editor to stop the debugger feature. Then, you can proceed to correct the error by adding another code line at the beginning of the existing code line. Here is an example:

  Dim X as Integer

Using the Debugger Settings

- Using this formula string is one way of correcting various Macro Errors. However, there is a much easier way to do this. You can use the debugger settings to do everything for you automatically. To activate this command, you can go through the following steps:
- First, go to the visual basic editor and place your cursor before the word private and press the function key F8.
- After this, you should press F8 about three more times.
- The runtime error should appear. This error code means that the range does not support the property or method used.

X = 2
Range ("A1").Valu = X
In this case, the problem is the spelling of Value. Using the debugger will be a great way to determine all the errors in your coding. It will also help you understand codes better in the coming days. This ultimate benefit is why you should use it as much as possible.

Additional Terms

Here are some other words that you need to remember when working with an Excel sheet:

- Variables: Values that are declared and executed within the program.

- Events: These refer to the executable actions that various users can apply using the program. Below are some examples:
- Summation
- Obtaining averages
- Finding solutions to algebraic formulas

The If-Then Statement

This condition is an explicit statement used to describe a situation wherein the specific conditions subject to the execution of a certain code line within Excel are fulfilled. This report will be useful for general presentations of flowcharts as well as graphs using Microsoft Excel in the future.

For example, we have this equation:

$$X+Y= XY; (X)(Y) = XY$$

This equation can be transformed into an if-then statement for Excel. The equation can be read as such: If X added to Y is equal to XY, then X multiplied to Y is also similar to XY.

This equation is also an example of the correlation between the variables within a cell. Using the formula bar, you can find out the mathematical relationship between the variables in each cell without having to go through the equation manually. All you have to do is to type in the proper formula, and you will eventually be able to yield the data that you need. This topic will further be discussed in the next few chapters of the book.

I hope that through these terms, you will further understand how the program works. I hope that you will also comprehend the usefulness of the program regarding the different computation and graphical representations. Now that you have a clearer concept as to the definition of the program, we will now go to the code or basic language used to create Excel. The VBA or the Visual Basic Application Code.

The VBA (Visual Basic Application) Code

Earlier, we discussed how to apply Visual Basic Application code when creating your own spreadsheet. However, you may be curious how the VBA code interacts with the spreadsheet in order to make it automated. This section will discuss how the VBA code links to the automation the program.

This particular system line provides interaction between the user and the interface through the intercession of the Excel Object Model. This particular model refers to a set of vocabulary identification modes along with programmed functions and methods that enabled the user to read and encode values through the program without difficulty.

As an example, customized toolbars or command bars, as well as easily readable message boxes, are integrated into the program to allow further interaction between the machine and the user. On the part of the user, he can then create commands that will trigger certain functions within the program, allowing them to get results efficiently and within seconds.

Because of this, the visual basic application has been truly deemed as a highly efficient and flexible program language that can be used in a variety of functions within a computer.

Excel and Other Programs: A Correlation

Now that you know the basic elements of the visual basic language, we can now proceed to discuss the application of the Excel program as it connects to other Microsoft Office applications.

Because of the visual basic language, Excel can perform other more complex operations that some other Microsoft programs are not able to do. For example, in an Excel spreadsheet, a user will be able to perform complex arithmetic operations using scientific formulas that would otherwise be difficult to solve manually.

In addition to this, the Excel spreadsheet is known to be extremely interactive. How so? It is interactive in the sense that it has an extremely user-friendly interface that is also highly customizable. This feature will permit any user can include or attach additional programs that can help make the navigation and operations easier in the long run.

Excel can also work correctly with other Microsoft Office programs such as Microsoft Word or PowerPoint. The connectivity makes for a highly functional and interactive computerized work program that has made life easier for people of all backgrounds around the world. From professionals to students and even homemakers, everyone can utilize Excel for a wide variety of tasks in and out of the office.

A Short History

Ever since the creation of the program, Excel has been supporting end user programming which allows the automation of repetitive tasks as well as functions that are mainly user-defined.

In earlier versions of Excel, these various roles and programs were written within a syntax to be executed in the confines of the macro sheet. The default file extension for Excel had been.XLM up until version 4.0. In the next few releases, (5.0 onwards) the visual basic application language was already in use. Nowadays, all versions of the program, including Excel 2010 are capable of running the XLM macro. However, users are highly discouraged by Microsoft from using this file extension.

The Creation and Use of Charts and Graphs

Aside from empirical values and mathematical formulas, this particular program is supportive of presentations using charts, graphs or histograms as well. These components can be attached to the current sheet, or the parts could be embedded in an entirely different table. It can also be added as a separate object from the file.

An advantage of using Excel as your mode of presentation is that the values within your graphs can easily be updated if you can alter the values within the cells. As an example, if you want to change the measurements of your design within the report itself, the change in measurements will affect the corresponding visual graph by automatically altering the shape of the object itself.

This event makes for an incredibly dynamic presentation indeed. It is something that you should consider using if you want to make your reports and presentations (whether for school or your job).

Data Storage

Specific Number of Rows and Columns

Various versions of Excel differ regarding the prescribed size of the datasets for each row. The standard would be at least 16,000 rows for about 214 columns. Later versions were able to accommodate more rows. (65,000 rows to about 256 columns)

Below are some of the accepted file formats that you can use in an Excel program. Make sure to use these extensions whenever you are going to create and save a file via Microsoft Excel. This way, you will not end up having rendering issues in the long run.

- Main File Format: Excel Spreadsheet

- Available Filename Extensions: Previous Versions: .xls

- Excel 2007: .xlsx, .xlsm, (.xlsb)

The .xls format apparently corresponds to the Excel binary file format. However, the Excel 2007 version uses a slightly different file format in the open XML format for Office. This change followed a somewhat less traditional XML version called the XML spreadsheet. It was first introduced to the public in Excel 2002.

Problems with Excel 2007

The current versions of Excel are known to support XML extensions. However, the program is still backward when it comes to offering support for the previous binary extension formats. Additionally, the older versions of Excel can open and read the following file extensions without a problem, unlike the 2007 version. This issue is why some computer experts tend to prefer the older versions of the program instead of the new one. That being said, using any specific programs would still be at your discretion.

- CSV
- DBF
- SYLK
- DIF

However, support from Excel 2007 was subsequently removed for older file formats. This issue occurs because most of the older file formats work with DOS based programs. These programs are not compatible with Microsoft Excel.

Deleting a Macro

When you feel like you are not going to be using a particular macro anymore, or if the macro you recorded previously is not quite what you expected, then you can just delete the macro. Follow these steps to delete the macro:

- Open the spreadsheet with the macro.
- If the macro is in the Personal Macro Workbook, then you have to unhide it first. Head to **View tab**, and click **Unhide** in the **Window** group.
- Click **Personal** under the **Unhide workbooks.**
- If it isn't already there, display the **Developer tab**.
- In the **Developer tab**, click on **Macros** under the **Code** group.
- A list called **Macros In** pops up. First, select the workbook which contains the macro you do not need any more.
- Select the name of the macro that you wish to delete in the **Macro name** box.
- Finally, delete the macro by clicking on **Delete** button.

Conclusion

Now that you have the basic idea of what Excel is, and how you can use it, you will now be able to create a spreadsheet, perform complex mathematical operations in it, and create beautiful charts that go hand-in-hand with the data you have presented. With the help of the different formatting options, you can also try and make your spreadsheet *look* better apart from just organizing it. Before you realize it, you are going to be creating spreadsheets with enormous amounts of data that would give even an expert a headache, and manage it with ease. The beauty of Excel is that you can work on certain parts of the data at a time, and because of its dynamic memory, you can use its results somewhere else.

Excel VBA, which is the programming language, is extremely powerful. Unlike traditional programming languages like Java, C, and C++, VBA is very easy to use, uses simple syntax that is more common sense than a format to be followed. It is because of VBA that Excel overpowered Lotus 1-2-3.

I hope this book was useful to you, and that you found the contents and examples easily understandable. Excel does not end with just these contents. It's an ocean, where you have to dive right in and see for yourself what it offers. But this book is enough to turn the beginner in you into an experienced Excel user with a clear understanding of the basic features of Excel. Excel will always be needed, as long as databases are present since with great amounts of data comes great responsibility to manage it.